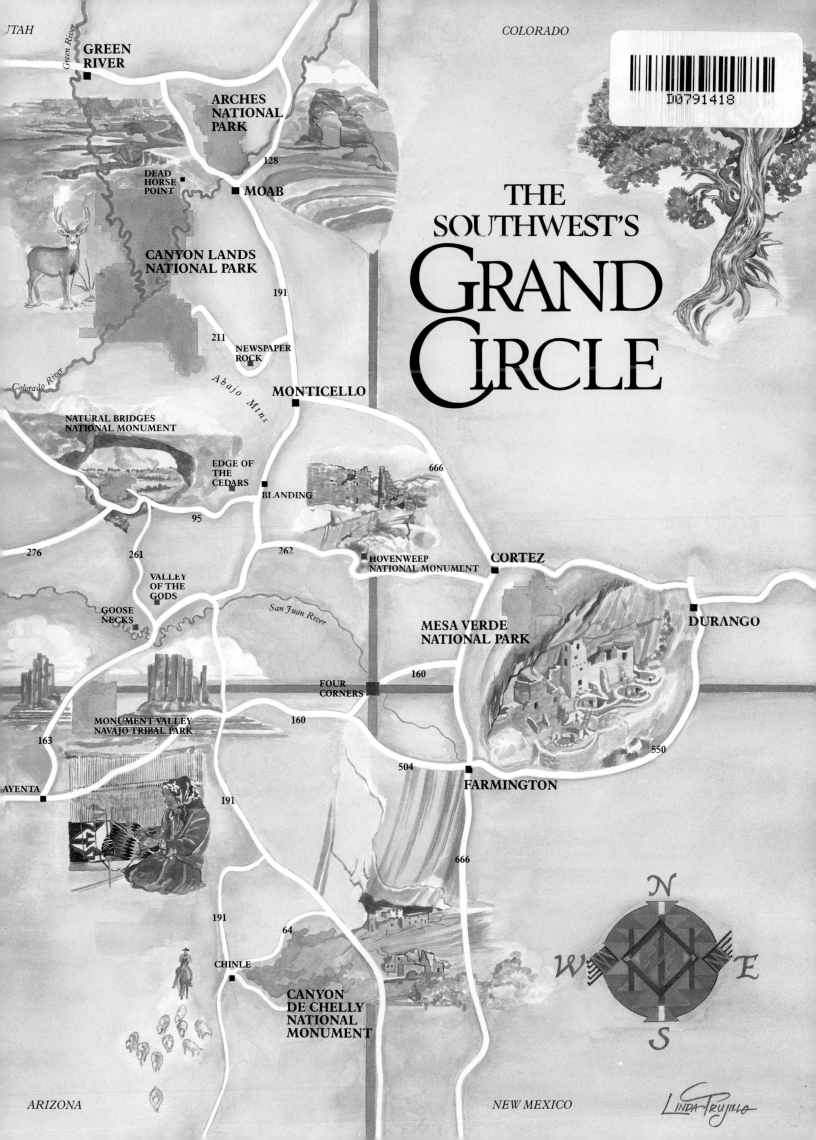

THE SOUTHWEST'S GRAND CIRCLE

UTAH

COLORADO

GREEN RIVER

ARCHES NATIONAL PARK

128

DEAD HORSE POINT

MOAB

CANYON LANDS NATIONAL PARK

191

211

NEWSPAPER ROCK

Colorado River

Abajo Mtns

MONTICELLO

NATURAL BRIDGES NATIONAL MONUMENT

EDGE OF THE CEDARS

BLANDING

666

95

276

261

262

HOVENWEEP NATIONAL MONUMENT

CORTEZ

VALLEY OF THE GODS

GOOSE NECKS

San Juan River

MESA VERDE NATIONAL PARK

DURANGO

FOUR CORNERS

160

MONUMENT VALLEY NAVAJO TRIBAL PARK

160

504

FARMINGTON

163

550

AYENTA

191

666

191

64

CHINLE

CANYON DE CHELLY NATIONAL MONUMENT

ARIZONA

NEW MEXICO

Linda Trujillo

N
W E
S

Rainstorm on the Grand Canyon's North Rim, from Cape Royal. CHRISTINE FANCHER

EXPLORING THE SOUTHWEST'S
GRAND CIRCLE

A Companion Press Book

by Mark A. Schlenz

©1988 Companion Press
Santa Barbara, California

Published in cooperation with the Grand Circle Association

With special thanks to Kit Law, Anne Markward,
the members of the Grand Circle Association,
and the dedicated staff of the National Parks,
National Monuments, State Parks and
recreational sites covered in this book.

Edited by Jane Freeburg

Designed by Linda Trujillo

Printed and bound in Korea

ISBN 0-944197-07-8

Fourth Printing
1991

CONTENTS

*Opposite: Flood-fluted walls of a
slickrock canyon.* ROBERT WINSLOW

Top: Utah juniper berries.
FRED HIRSCHMANN

Center: Spring leaves of box elder.
FRED HIRSCHMANN

*Bottom: Moonrise over
Hovenweep "Castle."* JERRY JACKA

CHAPTER ONE

Plateau Country — Discover the Grand Circle

The 1,400-mile adventure of the Southwest's Grand Circle explores some of the most spectacular country on earth — the incredible landscapes of the Colorado Plateaus. The route encircles America's highest concentration of scenic national parks and monuments, rugged mountains, deep canyons, skyward cliffs, prehistoric Indian ruins, nostalgic villages and other fascinating attractions. The Grand Circle overflows with natural wonders. It is an unparalleled vacationland containing seven national parks, seven national monuments, a Navajo tribal park and a variety of state parks and historic sites.

The Colorado Plateaus

Bordered on the south by the Sonoran and Painted Deserts, the Great Basin to the west, the Rocky Mountains to the east and the Uinta Mountains to the north, the Colorado Plateau region is an area where forces of water, wind and time have laid bare the rock history of the earth's ages in impressive geologic displays. Within the Grand Circle, elevations range from 2,000 feet above sea level at the bottom of the Grand Canyon to over 10,000 feet high on the plateaus of Southern Utah. Layers of rock exposed between these elevations tell the story of the ages as they are cut by deep gorges or sculpted into fantastic forms of mesas, buttes, monuments, spires, arches, bridges and eerie shapes called hoodoos.

Aeons ago this entire region was alternately flooded by shallow seas and smothered by wind-blown sand. Silts and materials deposited on the floors of ancient oceans compressed the drowned dunes of previous ages and were in turn compacted by the weight of later deserts. In subsequent periods, forces of continental drift created dramatic uplifting of the accumulated layers, raising some areas up to a mile above sea level and fracturing the sedimen-

Below: A Sego lily sends out a single blossom. CHUCK PLACE

Opposite: A broad sweep of the Colorado River in Canyonlands National Park. GARY LADD

Bottom left: Colorful desert life — a collared lizard, Arches National Park. CHUCK PLACE

Bottom center: Golden autumn Buckthorn foliage. FRED HIRSCHMANN

Bottom right: Lichen and desert varnish, patina on Navajo Sandstone. FRED HIRSCHMANN

tary layers with faults and joints. Volcanic materials also began to work upward, spreading molten lava in some regions and creating bulges — the Abajo, Henry and La Sal mountains — in surface layers where they did not break through. As the seas retreated far from the elevated region, tremendous rivers from melting glaciers in the north began to carve the land. River courses and erosion from wind and rain continue to create the landscape of today's great Southwest.

Much of the story in stone is told by fossilized records of prehistoric plants, dinosaurs and other animals inhabiting the region through the ages. Largely stripped of surface soils, the naked landscapes of the Colorado plateaus allow insights into the life of past ages while continuing to host a surprising variety of thriving species.

Pinyon-juniper forests are common on the plateaus. Pinyon pines and Utah junipers are mixed with sages and other brushes, greasewood, Mormon tea, desert holly, cliff rose, saltbush, snakeweed, cacti, yucca and a variety of grasses. Lizards, snakes, amphibians and numerous bird species live in these plant communities. Mammals found here range in size from mice, squirrels, rabbits and skunks to ringtailed cats, foxes, bobcats, coyotes, mule deer, bighorn sheep, pronghorn antelope and a few pumas and bears. At slightly higher elevations, Gambel's oak forests intermingle with mountain mahogany, manzanita and several species of berries. High in the mountains, quaking aspens are found among spruce and fir.

Life in the hot and arid Southwest constantly challenges plants and animals as well as humans. Historic traces of man's struggle to survive in this environment are numerous, as are examples of old ways of life being maintained into modern times.

Strange markings — called pictographs and petroglyphs — painted or etched on rocks and canyon walls communicate the passing of ancient Anasazi and Fremont cultures which mysteriously disappeared from the region around 1250 AD. Ruins of impressive centers of Anasazi civilizations still stand in the dramatic settings of Mesa Verde, Hovenweep, Canyon de Chelly and Navajo National Monument. Traditional Native American lifestyles continue to be reflected in the architecture and arts and crafts of the region. Visits to Canyon de Chelly or the Navajo tribal park at Monument Valley provide picturesque glimpses into the continuation of a fascinating culture.

Exploring the Circle

Landscapes of the Colorado Plateaus are filled with amazing diversity. From riverbottoms of ancient bare rock at the bottom of the mile-deep Grand Canyon to spring blossomings of wildflowers high in alpine meadows, from imagination-stirring silhouettes of towering formations shaped by nature to the artistry of vanished peoples speaking silently from stony surfaces, the Grand Circle presents an overwhelming variety of adventures and experiences.

Thanks to a well-planned, all-weather highway system, the Grand Circle may be toured in one complete circuit or explored in smaller segments. Each mile of road gives access to the beauty and splendor of the region and offers spectacular photo opportunities. Restaurants, services and accommodations are readily available. A Grand Circle adventure can start and end at any point; however, a perfect starting point is one of the true wonders of the world, the Grand Canyon.

CHAPTER TWO

Time and the River

A walk from the rim to the Inner Gorge of the Grand Canyon is a walk through geologic time. The primeval streams that are today's rivers began millions of years ago to sculpt and shape this country of canyons. Each season the elements stole a share of the soil and carried it far away to the sea, as now the great Colorado River and its tributaries scour the canyons of the Southwest for grains of rock to carry to the Gulf of California. Layers of the earth's history are exposed, the ages and stages laid bare to the delight of the geologist, photographer and everyday traveler through nature's art gallery.

The canyon walls echo the sounds of water, wind and the animals who live at the heart of the river. Amid the rapids caused by debris washed down side canyons, the echo becomes a roar. Above the Glen Canyon Dam, where man has harnessed the river's power, the glassy surface of Lake Powell reflects the azure of the sky and golds, reds and purples of the shadowed sandstone. It takes more time than we can imagine to create such beauty — time, and the river.

Opposite: Colors of a Grand Canyon sunset, from Hopi Point. ED COOPER

Above: The Kaibab trail twists its way past O'Neill Butte, Grand Canyon National Park. GARY LADD

The Grand Canyon's South Rim

Grand Canyon National Park preserves one of the world's most spectacular examples of a river's canyon-carving power. Here, the Colorado River has cut a chasm 277 river-miles long and about a mile deep into the Kaibab Plateau. Today, forces of the rushing river, wind, rain, snow, frost and the sun's heat are still at work sculpting the Grand Canyon. Erosion has left the artistry of subtly hued rock in a deep and challenging abyss that never fails to inspire awe in viewers who gravitate here from around the globe.

We know ancient peoples lived in this amazing landscape. Over 2,500 prehistoric sites — mute testimony of their passing — have been recorded throughout Grand Canyon National Park. Contemporary Indian tribes live in the area as well: Havasupai, Hualapai and Navajo reservations are adjacent to park boundaries. Don Lopez de Cardenas, a Captain in Coronado's expedition of 1540, was the first European to record his impressions of the

Above: Twin rainbows and Isis Temple, from Hopi Point.
LARRY ULRICH

Opposite: Elves Chasm, a grotto deep in the Grand Canyon.
LARRY ULRICH

canyon blocking his search for gold: he found it impassable but impressive.

Major John Wesley Powell made the first of two geologic research expeditions down the Colorado River in 1869 with four wooden boats, a crew of nine and the goal to chart, measure and name the canyons and creeks of the mighty Colorado. A determined one-armed adventurer, Powell described his discoveries and hardships in evocative prose. Thomas Moran's paintings, inspired by photographs taken during the Powell expeditions, helped convince Congress to establish Grand Canyon as a national park in 1919.

The adventurous who heard about the Grand Canyon were determined to see it: flocks of travelers appeared by stage, horseback or muleback — with a number of prospectors on foot or by burro. In Grand Canyon Village, early tourism development included a Santa Fe Railway Station built in 1901, curio shops and the Kolb Brothers' photography studio, established in 1904. The historic El Tovar Hotel and Bright Angel Lodge were part of the early Fred Harvey Company's western expansion of the hospitality industry, as were rim-side buildings designed to blend with the natural scene by architect Mary Jane Coulter. Many of these early structures are now on the National Register of Historic Places.

Top: Claret cup cactus blooms.
CHUCK PLACE

Middle: Kaibab century plant rosette. FRED HIRSCHMANN

Bottom: Sedimentary layers of Kaibab limestone. ED COOPER

Opposite: View from the Grand Canyon's South Rim at Mojave Point. ED COOPER

A Dry Land of Subtle Riches

About 15 inches of scant annual rainfall on the Canyon's South Rim supports gnarled pinyon pines and junipers, clinging to the lichen-painted rocks. Seeking slightly more moisture, ponderosa pine stand back from the rim, mingled with Gambel oaks; a quiet Douglas fir forest is a special attraction on the East Rim Drive.

In spite of a dry environment, Grand Canyon's wildlife is rich and diverse. Ravens, turkey vultures, violet-green swallows and swifts soar or dive in canyon updrafts. Small rodents — the Abert tassel-eared squirrel, rock squirrels, chipmunks — are at home in the rocky crevices. Mule deer, gray foxes and coyotes also live here, as do elusive mountain lions and bobcats.

The National Park Service Visitor Center at Grand Canyon Village — open daily all year — is a good first stop for an orientation slide show, information on activities and a current schedule of interpretive programs. At *Mather Point*, named for the first head of the National Park Service, many visitors have their initial view of the breathtaking Grand Canyon. The Colorado River, about one mile below and 300 feet wide, looks like a tiny, silvery line. *Yavapai Point* is the location of Yavapai Museum, where an excellent display explains the geologic history of the canyon. The glass-walled museum is an excellent place to watch summer lightning storms or snow on the North Rim in winter.

There are many more ways to see the Grand Canyon — a mule ride or steep hike into its heart, a river adventure on the Colorado, an aerial view by helicopter or small plane — the vast landscape demands much of the viewer. Most visitors are drawn to the ever-changing panorama unfolding from the rim.

Past the Lodge area, West Rim Drive skirts the rim of the Grand Canyon and offers a number of viewpoints. Two trail-view overlooks, Maricopa Point and Powell Memorial, offer vistas of the canyon and the inviting trails below. From Hopi Point, just one mile beyond, a long section of the Colorado River is visible. At Mojave Point,

if the air is still, sounds of crashing waves at Hermit Rapids a mile below may be audible. The Abyss offers a view into, rather than across, the Canyon — the eroded Bright Angel Shale of Great Mojave Wall has left a steep, breathtaking glimpse down into the rock. West Rim Drive viewpoints, even Hermits Rest at the road's end, are popular with photographers eager to capture the delicate lights and shadows of canyon sunsets.

The South Rim Nature Trail hugs the Canyon's edge from Mather Point to Hermits Rest; any section of the walk is a pleasant alternative to the eight-mile West Rim Drive. Self-guiding trail booklets are available. Past Grand Canyon Village and Mather Point, East Rim Drive is a 23-mile adventure through forest and high rim country with panoramic views between. The popular South Kaibab Trail begins near Yaki Point; it descends into the Canyon, crosses the Colorado River and climbs up the other side to the North Rim.

Landscape painter Thomas Moran returned repeatedly to paint the Grand Canyon; *Moran Point* is named in his honor. One of Moran's favorite views was Red Canyon, a vividly-colored slash of Hakatai Shale seen to the west. At *Tusayan Ruin*, an Anasazi pueblo inhabited about 1185 AD has been excavated. The adjacent museum includes exhibits on Indian cultures of the Grand Canyon area. Desert View is furthest east of the Grand Canyon National Park overlooks. The river is glimpsed among sloping cliffs; buttes and temples of rock across the canyon hint at another world below. A spiral staircase in the picturesque stone watchtower leads to a viewing platform.

From Grand Canyon National Park's East Entrance Station, Highway 64 leads east to views of the Painted Desert along Highway 89. The eroded canyon rims of the Little Colorado River, on its way to join the Colorado for the journey through the Grand Canyon, cut into the expanse of Navajo lands.

Above: Stone watchtower over the Colorado River from Desert View. ED COOPER

Left: Timeless terraces created by weather and river, Grand Canyon National Park. RICK McINTYRE

Opposite, above: Vista from Desert View at sunset. DAN PEHA

Inset: Murals in Desert View Watchtower, by Hopi artist Fred Kabotie. ED COOPER

Opposite, below: The Colorado River carves through Marble Canyon. ED COOPER

Marble Canyon

State Highway 89A leads north along the Echo Cliffs to cross the Colorado River at Navajo Bridge, a 616-foot arched span almost 500 feet above the current. A few miles above the bridge is historic Lees Ferry, where Grand Canyon National Park begins. This is Mile 0 for the river runners who begin float trips down the mighty Colorado.

Downstream from Navajo Bridge is Marble Gorge, where the Colorado River winds through polished limestone cliffs that inspired explorer John Wesley Powell to name this marvel "Marble Canyon." There is no marble here, but the 60-plus river-miles leading to the confluence of the mighty Colorado and its tributary, the Little Colorado, are the exclusive delight of those traveling by boat. The adventure of Marble Gorge includes verdant springs, the rush of rapids and majestic eroded cliffs framing slices of sky above.

Lake Powell and Glen Canyon National Recreation Area

Upstream from Lees Ferry near the town of Page, Arizona is the Glen Canyon Dam. A massive concrete structure built between 1956 and 1964, the dam turns the current of the Colorado River into hydroelectric power — and creates the recreational playground of Lake Powell. With nearly 2,000 miles of shoreline, Lake Powell is one of the world's largest man-made lakes; the three million visitors it hosts each year make it one of the most popular sites in the Grand Circle.

Lake Powell is named for John Wesley Powell, whose scientific expeditions of the Green and Colorado Rivers brought him to this area in 1869. Powell named the canyon here for the lush glens that adorned the riverside. Earlier explorers, accompanying Fathers Escalante and Dominguez in 1776, found the environment less hospitable; they struggled to ford the river, finally chopping steps for their pack train in the sandstone walls at Padre Creek. Their ford became known as the "Crossing of the

Fathers," now under the waters of Lake Powell but still commemorated by Padre Bay and Dominguez Butte. Lake Powell's lure is its colorful rocky scenery — and miles of solitary shoreline protected by Glen Canyon National Recreation Area. There are endless side canyons to explore, fishing holes to discover, changing reflections of rock formations in the still water, silhouettes of buttes and peaks in the evening sky. The lake offers year-round dry, clear, sunny Southwestern warmth — it is ideal to explore by houseboat, and local marinas offer comfortably appointed houseboats of various sizes.

Lakeside camping, fishing, waterskiing, photography and boat tours are all popular pursuits at Lake Powell. A good map will open many possibilities for discovery hikes in the side canyons of Glen Canyon National Recreation Area. Sheer walls of rock, shady canyons with delicate hanging gardens, natural arches, water-carved bridges of stone, and Anasazi ruins might be seen by hikers.

Rainbow Bridge National Monument

Lake Powell's waters make one of the most beautiful sights in the Glen Canyon area accessible by boat. The Navajo call 290-foot Rainbow Bridge Nonne-Zoshi, "rainbow of stone." Its graceful shape is majestically clear against the blue skies, and often reflected in the slice of lake below its span. Rainbow Bridge was formed by water flowing from nearby Navajo Mountain down Bridge Creek to the Colorado River. Erosion of the soft Navajo Sandstone at the top curve of the bridge and the harder Kayenta Formation at its base combined with huge breaking slabs of stone to gradually sculpt the bridge.

Rainbow Bridge can also be reached by foot or horseback from Navajo Mountain Trading Post (14 miles), or by the hiking trail from abandoned Rainbow Lodge (13 miles). Spring and fall are the best times to make this trek through the canyons at the base of Navajo Mountain. The routes lead through the Navajo Reservation and a hiking permit from the Navajo tribe is required. Camping and supplies are not available at Rainbow Bridge National Monument, though campgrounds are located along the Rainbow Lodge and Navajo Mountain trails. Be sure to carry adequate drinking water.

Opposite, top: Mesas and buttes rise beyond Padre Bay, Lake Powell. GARY LADD

Opposite, below: Houseboating near La Gorce Arch. JERRY JACKA

Above: Rainbow Bridge, reflected in the still waters of Lake Powell. GARY LADD

Right: Wahweap Marina and Lodge. DEL WEBB CORP.

CHAPTER THREE

The Grand Staircase

Rising 6,000 feet above the canyon-carving waters of the Colorado River, the Kaibab Plateau forms the north rim of the Grand Canyon. The Kaibab Plateau itself lies near the base of a climbing succession of cliffs and plateaus sometimes called the Grand Staircase. From the ancient rocks of the Vishnu Schist — the oldest sedimentary layer revealed at the bottom of the Grand Canyon — to the rim of the Markagunt Plateau at Cedar Breaks, nearly two vertical miles and two billion years of the earth's geology are exposed. Broken edges of successive layers of rock strata, uplifted and tilted northward, are displayed in the Vermilion Cliffs near Pipe Spring National Monument, the towering White Cliffs of Navajo Sandstone at Zion and the Pink Cliffs of Bryce Canyon and Cedar Breaks. Each step up the Grand Staircase into higher elevations introduces different plant communities and varied animal species. Climbing the Grand Staircase is a wonderful way to become acquainted with the diverse range of geologic layers — as well as the botany and the wildlife — found throughout the Southwest's Grand Circle.

Opposite: October colors near Bright Angel Point, Grand Canyon's North Rim. TOM BEAN

Above: Collage of leafy color on the North Rim forest floor. GEORGE H. H. HUEY

Houserock Valley

After crossing Navajo Bridge at Marble Canyon, US 89A follows the Vermilion Cliffs and enters the wide sweep of Houserock Valley. Named by early travelers who found shelter where two huge rocks had fallen together, the valley is full of animal life — including a protected herd of buffalo. From Houserock Valley, the Kaibab Plateau looms prominently on the landscape.

Grand Canyon National Park, North Rim

The Kaibab Plateau takes its name from the Paiute word meaning "mountain lying down." Bordering the North Rim of the Grand Canyon for over 200 miles, the tremendous expanse of this plateau reaches elevations of up to 9,000 feet. Nearly 2,000 feet higher in places than the canyon's southern rim, the Kaibab receives in-

Top: The sharp spire of Mt. Hayden from Point Imperial. GARY LADD

Below: The tassel-eared Kaibab squirrel. MICHAEL H. FRANCIS

creased precipitation — nearly 11 feet of snow each winter — and supports a large virgin ponderosa pine forest that has never been logged. Isolated — like an island in the sky — the Kaibab Plateau provides habitat for majestic eagles and falcons as well as the Grand Canyon's unique "tassel-eared," white-tailed Kaibab squirrel.

Separated from the South Rim by the Grand Canyon itself and situated at the base of the Grand Staircase, the North Rim is remote, though by no means inaccessible. Highway 67, leaving 89A at the junction near Jacob Lake, is the scenic Kaibab Plateau-North Rim Parkway. It travels 43 miles through coniferous forests, flowering open meadows and shallow sinkhole lakes of the high Kaibab Plateau to the Grand Canyon's isolated northern rim. The secluded, cool North Rim receives only 10% of the park's total visitation, and is a quiet alternative for those wishing for the solitude to listen to wind whispering across the distances of mountains lying down.

Though at night the lights at the South Rim, 11 air-miles away, are often visible from North Rim's Grand Canyon Lodge, the distance by road is 214 miles to Grand Canyon Village. During the open season — usually from mid-May to late October — services at the North Rim include a general store, a gasoline station and a campground. Accommodations are available at the Grand Canyon Lodge, a historic landmark situated for optimum views near the tip of Bright Angel Point.

Three other particularly scenic overlooks at the North Rim are — from east to west — Point Imperial, Cape Royal and Point Sublime. Near Cape Royal, Angel's Window frames views of the Colorado River a mile below. Other roadside overlooks include Painted Desert Viewpoint and Vista Encantadora. The North Kaibab Trail descends into the canyon from the North Rim while the Widforss Trail winds through the forests along the rim, a round trip of 10 miles.

Just before Highway 89A leaves the Kaibab National Forest at the northern edge of the Kaibab Plateau, there is an excellent Forest Service viewpoint from which to observe the climbing bands of the Chocolate, Vermilion, White and Pink Cliffs of the Grand Staircase ascending into the higher plateaus of the north.

Pipe Spring National Monument

The route up the Grand Staircase continues north and west on Highway 89 to the junction with 389 at Fredonia, Arizona, then west on 389 across the Kaibab-Paiute Indian Reservation surrounding Pipe Spring National Monument. Legend attributes the name Pipe Spring to early Mormon explorers camped by the spring at the base of the Vermilion Cliffs; according to the story, a young man was teased into proving his marksmanship by shooting out the bottom of a pipe bowl at fifty paces.

The old stone fort at Pipe Spring was built by Mormon Pioneers in the 1860s as a refuge for farming and ranching families during times of Indian troubles. The Pipe Spring oasis was also used as a base of operations for Major John Wesley Powell's geologic and anthropological surveys of the Colorado Plateaus. Powell, the daring scientific explorer who first descended the Colorado River, was also instrumental in negotiating a peace between the Mormons and Ute Indians.

Pipe Spring was declared a National Monument by President Warren G. Harding on May 31, 1923 to commemorate the struggle for exploration and settlement of the Southwest. A living history program recreates spinning, weaving, baking arts and other aspects of pioneer life. Self-guided and conducted tours around the fort and interpretive exhibits are available as well.

Zion National Park

On a higher step of the Grand Staircase is Zion National Park. Here, the Virgin River has cut a canyon through a nearly 2,000 foot deep geologic layer of petrified dunes known as Navajo Sandstone. Paiute Indians called the canyon of the Virgin River Ioogoon, their word for arrow quiver, which meant the canyon was a place that must be exited by the same route it was entered. The Paiutes told stories about mischievous spirits among the rock formations and would not enter the canyon alone or remain there after dark. It was an early Mormon settler who first saw "temples built by hands not of man" in the canyon's towering masses of stone and said, "I shall call this place Little Zion."

From the west, Zion National Park is approached through the town of Hurricane and Highway 9 to Springdale. Just beyond the National Park Service Visitor Center, located at the bases of the West Temple and the Towers of the Virgin, is the turn-off for a six-mile scenic drive into the depths of the canyon. Pull-outs at Zion Lodge and the Grotto Picnic Area are wonderful lunch stops and provide access for day-hiking trails to The Court of the Patriarchs, Weep-

Top left: Wagons and historic stone fort at Pipe Spring National Monument. GARY LADD

Top right: In the Court of the Patriarchs — Abraham, Isaac and Jacob — Zion National Park. LARRY ULRICH

Above: Zion's West Temple and the Towers of the Virgin. CHRISTINE FANCHER

23

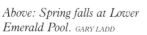

Above: Spring falls at Lower Emerald Pool. GARY LADD

Inset: Winter at Weeping Rock. CHRISTINE FANCHER

Top: Zion Canyon and the Virgin River from Angels Landing trail viewpoint. FRANK S. BALTHIS

Opposite, top: Mountain forests above the multi-hued amphitheater of "the breaks." CHRISTINE FANCHER

Opposite, below: Flower-carpeted alpine meadows at Cedar Breaks National Monument. LARRY ULRICH

ing Rock and the Emerald Pools. Past Angels Landing, the Great White Throne and The Organ, the road ends at the Temple of Sinawava. From here, a handicap-accessible, one-mile nature trail leads to the Gateway to the Narrows — an impressive gorge carved by the Virgin River — less than 20 feet wide, yet in places 2,000 feet deep.

Zion National Park's East Entrance is located in a picturesque region of slickrock where stone pillars have been weirdly eroded into hoodoos and where different geologic forces have created the combined horizontal and vertical crossbedding seen in Checkerboard Mesa. Between Zion Canyon and the East Entrance, the Park road travels through tunnels hewn in the rock — a remarkable

feat of road building completed in 1930. From the east end of the Mt. Carmel Tunnel, a short trail leads to the dramatic Canyon Overlook, one of the few places in Zion National Park where the view is pulled downward across the mouth of Zion Canyon to the majestically-named formations that guard the Virgin River.

In the more remote northwestern corner of Zion National Park, just off Interstate 15, another scenic drive climbs to an overlook of the Finger Canyons of the Kolob. The drive is just 10 miles round-trip and well worth the time spent watching the rock formations glide past. A self-guided auto tour booklet is available from the Kolob Visitor Center. At Lee Pass, a trail leads seven miles to a view of massive Kolob Arch — at a span of 310 feet, the largest free-standing arch in the world.

Zion National Park, with its evocatively-named formations, is one of the best places to watch the light change on the faces of the rock. Spring wildflowers and wildlife abound here. Park naturalists offer walking tours and evening programs for visitors from late March until early November; Zion is tempting in the less-crowded late fall and winter. In September, Zion is the location of Utah's annual Folk Life Festival. Nearby Springdale offers the multi-media spectacular "The Grand Circle" — outdoors among the whispering rock giants at the O.C. Tanner Amphitheater.

Cedar Breaks

Near the top of the Grand Staircase, at 10,400 feet on the rim of the Markagunt Plateau, the world seems to drop off suddenly into a gigantic multi-hued amphitheater. Twenty-five hundred feet deep and three miles from rim to rim, this natural basin covers 75% of the 6,155 acres at Cedar Breaks National Monument. The amphitheater is filled with majestic spires, grotesque columns and graceful arches shaped by weather-eroded limestone of the Wasatch Formation. Colorful reds and purples are created by small amounts of iron and other minerals in the soil which oxidize when exposed by erosion to the atmosphere. "Breaks" is a word commonly used by early settlers to refer to badlands, eroded landscapes with little or no vegetation. These same settlers mistakenly referred to Utah juniper trees as "cedars," and first called this incredible amphitheater Cedar Breaks.

The higher elevations at Cedar Breaks host a variety of high forest and alpine plant communities. Here, 1,600-year-old ancient Bristlecone Pines, perhaps the oldest living things on earth, cling tenaciously to the

Above: Hikers among Bryce's weathered limestone formations.
CHUCK PLACE

windswept ridges of Cedar Breaks. Midsummer brings a brilliant variety of wildflowers, their colors gracing the alpine meadows along the plateau rim. Nearby, 11,307-foot Brianhead Peak was created by volcanic activity, as were the nearby cinder cones which play an important role in creating this landscape. In these high elevations, lava flows are sometimes surrounded by aspen and fir forests. Animals seen at Cedar Breaks include red squirrels, porcupines and marmots; watch for signs of the elusive pika along the Alpine Pond trail. Many birds — including the noisy Clark's nutcracker — are frequent visitors to the campground and picnic areas which are open from late June through September. In winter, Cedar Breaks is blanketed with eight to ten feet of snow — ideal for cross-country skiing and views of the snow-dusted formations. Alpine and Nordic skiing are popular at nearby Brianhead ski resort.

A number of self-guiding rim and forest trails explore the Monument. A six-mile paved road winds along the rim through fields and forests offering viewpoints of the breaks. The picturesque Cedar Breaks Visitor Center was built by the Civilian Conservation Corps in 1938 — lava rock for the fireplace was hauled from Brianhead Mountain.

Among the magnificent vistas from the high rim of the Markagunt Plateau at Cedar Breaks is a view eastward along the Pink Cliffs to the Paunsaugunt Plateau where more awe-inspiring amphitheaters break away at Bryce Canyon.

Bryce Canyon

The Paunsaugunt Plateau sits at slightly lower elevations than Cedar Breaks, but Bryce Canyon has many of the same plant and animal species as its neighbor at the top of the Pink Cliffs of the Grand Staircase — including rare pumas, elk and black bear. Fifteen million years of uplifts and faults in the earth's crust have created the magnificent amphitheaters of Bryce with their brightly colored limestone pinnacles, spires and canyon walls eroded from ancient lakebed deposits. Like the landscape at Cedar Breaks, the amphitheaters at Bryce were carved by thousands of rivulets, tiny streams fed by snowmelt and thundershowers draining the basin from

Above: Bryce Canyon's "red rocks standing like men in a bowl-shaped canyon." LOU SWENSON

Right: Oxidizing minerals, exposed by erosion, help create Bryce's palette of colors. DAN PEHA

Far right: A gnarled pine in The Queens Garden. CHUCK PLACE

Above: View from Inspiration Point. JOHN VAVRUSKA

Right: Delicately-colored formations of Bryce Canyon. ROBERT WINSLOW

Opposite: Zion Overlook on Hwy 14 — fall colors from atop the Grand Staircase. CHRISTINE FANCHER

Inset: A curious, big-eared doe. Mule deer are found throughout the Grand Circle. TOM BEAN

the plateau rim to the Paria River two thousand feet below. Winter freezing and thawing cycles "frost wedge" the rock, splitting off large chunks.

The intricate shapes and hues of Bryce Canyon have a profound effect on the imagination. Paiute Indians called Bryce by a word which translates simply as "red rocks standing like men in a bowl-shaped canyon." Mormon settler Ebenezer Bryce, who once tried to scratch out a living here and gave his name to the location, described the canyon as "a hell of a place to lose a cow." Modern visitors conjure all sorts of images of minarets, pagodas and even "platoons of Turkish soldiers in pantaloons" in the other-worldly magnificence and infinite variety of Bryce Canyon.

Visitors can view the diverse colors and formations of Bryce by driving the 21-mile paved road connecting fantastic overviews including Fairyland, Sunset Point and Inspiration Point. The vibrant, clear sky at Bryce usually allows distant vistas of the Table Cliffs of the Aquarius Plateau to the northeast, the Kaibab Plateau to the south and the 85-mile distant dome of Navajo Mountain.

Open year-round, Bryce Canyon has hiking trails both along the canyon rim and descending to its bottom. Consider joining a moonlight hike, viewing spectacular night skies or attending campfire programs on summer evenings. In winter, check out a pair of snowshoes from the Visitor's Center and explore the crimson, gold and glittering white landscape from the rim.

CHAPTER FOUR

A Wilderness of Rocks

East of the Grand Staircase the wide expanses of southern Utah reach out across seemingly endless miles of exposed, bare, windswept rock. These are the canyonlands, the heart of the slickrock region of the Colorado Plateaus. Though canyons are characteristic features throughout the Southwest's Grand Circle, nowhere do they dominate the landscape as they do in the plateau heartland. This is true canyon country; deep chasms of the Green, the Escalante, the Dirty Devil and the San Juan Rivers channel their torrents through arid deserts of stone until they join the most impressive canyon-carver of all, the mighty Colorado River. Explorer Major John Wesley Powell wrote of this landscape: "Wherever we look there is but a wilderness of rocks; deep gorges, where the rivers are lost below cliffs and towers and pinnacles; and ten thousand strangely carved forms in every direction." This is the famous red rock country where Butch Cassidy once hid in his "Robber's Roost" and where modern travelers may still lose their city cares in a fantasy of space and stone — in a wilderness of rocks.

Calf Creek

Between Bryce Canyon and Capitol Reef National Parks lies the still-wild Escalante River. As yet undammed, the Escalante is crossed by only one road: the low bridge on Highway 12 near Calf Creek Recreation Area. Nestled deep in the beautiful canyon of the Escalante, the small, picturesque campground at Calf Creek is an excellent point-of-departure for expeditions down the untamed river. For the less adventurous, a well-marked nature path leads 2½ miles to the exquisite Lower Calf Creek Falls.

Anasazi Indian Village

Traveling north, Highway 12 climbs out of rugged Escalante Canyon to the base of Boulder Mountain. Here, the archaeological site and museum at Anasazi Indian Village State Park provides an enlightening glimpse into the lives of ancient

peoples who inhabited this wilderness of rock as far back as 1050 AD. Anasazi Indian Village was excavated by the University of Utah in 1958 as part of the Glen Canyon salvage project and was developed in 1970 by the Utah Division of Parks and Recreation. Visitors can inspect the actual village site and most of the uncovered artifacts which are on display in the museum.

Continuing north on Highway 12 between Boulder and Grover, the road climbs Boulder Mountain to an elevation of of 9,200 feet where golden eagles soar over aspen and spruce forests. Strategic look-out points along the way allow travelers splendid previews of the geologic wonderland of the Waterpocket Fold in Capitol Reef National Park miles to the east.

Capitol Reef National Park

In addition to the exciting scenic route over Boulder Mountain, Capitol Reef National Park may be reached from either the east or west on Highway 24, though the approach from the west perhaps offers the most startling introduction to the nearly 1,000-foot-thick sandstone escarpment of the reef. Once in the park, however, wonderful panoramas are everywhere. Capitol Reef takes its name from domed formations in the Waterpocket Fold reminiscent of our nation's capitol building. The Waterpocket Fold is a 100-mile-long stone bulge in the earth's crust containing small, eroded pockets that held rainwater for thirsty wayfarers. The colorfully-striped Chinle Formation that sprawls along the base of the Wingate sandstone cliffs inspired Indian peoples to call the country "Land of the Sleeping Rainbow."

From the ideally-situated National Park Service Visitor Center and campground to the terminus of the 25-mile scenic automobile drive — to the countless paths and routes into the contorted geology of the Waterpocket Fold — nature's incredible artistry is on exhibit at Capitol Reef National Park. Henry David Thoreau once said, "The finest workers in stone are not copper or steel tools, but the gentle touches of air and water working at their leisure with a liberal allowance of time." Sculptors wind and rain have been creating magnificent statuary at Capitol Reef for aeons.

Man has also left artistic touches on Capitol Reef. Fremont Indians, distant relatives of the Anasazi, inhabited this region from the seventh to the thirteenth centuries and carved outlines of bighorn sheep and other figures — called petroglyphs — into rock faces. By etching their imaginations on canyon walls, the Fremonts have communed with the earth, with the spirit world, and with people who came after.

Mormon settlers came to the Capitol Reef area in the 1880s and planted orchards along the Fremont River. No more than 10 families at any one time lived in this self-sufficient rural community, called Fruita for its abundant fruit harvests. Today, the Park Service maintains nearly 2,500 fruit trees as part of the historic landscape. The Benhuin family cabin and Fruita school house bear testimony to a vanished way of life.

In 1937, prompted by far-sighted local citizens, President Franklin D. Roosevelt established a small national monument at Capitol Reef. A greatly expanded national park was established in 1971. Park visitors can explore miles of backcountry jeep roads, contemplate the textures of changing light from Panorama Point or join the annual fruit harvest.

Goblin Valley State Park

Northeast of Capitol Reef National Park is the hidden mystery of Goblin Valley. This arid valley is a showcase of geologic history, and home to thousands of eroded Entrada Sandstone sculptures. These eerie formations can take on the haunting — and sometimes amusing — appearances of every fantasy creature from elephants to dolls to mushroom-headed monsters. The "goblins" are formed where layers of resistant siltstones alternate with more easily eroded shales.

Located just off Highway 24, the Visitor Center at Goblin Valley is open year-round to enhance visitor enjoyment of this rocky fantasyland. A campground and miles of tempting dirt roads are within the park. Goblin Valley is a wonderful place to rest from traveling — and exercise the imagination.

Opposite, top: The Waterpocket Fold, from Strike Valley Overlook. GARY LADD

Opposite, bottom: Colorful formations and cottonwoods in "the land of the sleeping rainbow." LARRY ULRICH

Above left: Eroded sandstone "goblins" and the Henry Mountains, Goblin Valley State Reserve. LARRY ULRICH

Top: Chimney Rock, Capitol Reef National Park. LARRY ULRICH

Arches
National Park

*Above: Landscape Arch, a ribbon
of stone spanning 291 feet.*
RICHARD WESTON

*Below left: Sunlit fins in the Fiery
Furnace.* RICK McINTYRE

*Below right: Sky-scraping forma-
tion in Park Avenue, Arches
National Park.* MAXINE CASS

*Opposite: Distant horizon beyond
Turret Arch, seen through the
North Window.* PAT O'HARA

*Opposite, below: Delicate Arch
and the La Sal Mountains.*
LARRY ULRICH

The distant La Sal Mountains — often
white with snow — provide a scenic
background for a stunning gallery of Nature's red rock sculpture at Arches National
Park. In addition to impressive arrays of
spires, fins, pinnacles and balanced rocks,
this unique geologic setting contains the
highest concentration of natural sandstone
arches in the world. How many arches? An
exact answer depends on definitions of an
"arch," but at least 200 openings ranging
from three-foot-wide windows in rock to
the 291-foot-span of Landscape Arch have
been catalogued in the 114-square-mile
Park.

New arches are still being formed
today by weathering forces of water, ice,
desert heat and wind that have been at
work on this landscape for ages. Skyline
Arch, seen from the road near Devil's
Garden, was once known as "Arch in the
Making," but in 1940 its opening was
suddenly enlarged to twice its former size
when a huge block of stone — its supports
gradually eroded grain by grain — finally
broke away from the fin.

Visitors can view many of the impressive arches — including the frequently
photographed Delicate Arch — from the
Park's 21-mile paved road and overlook
system. Physical scale can be deceiving in
country this big, however; a little distance
can make these huge formations appear
quite small compared to their actual pro-
portions. The entire landscape may seem
dramatically altered by taking even a few
steps. Short paths and trails lead from the

road right up to and under Double Arch, Turret Arch and the North and South Windows. Devil's Garden is the end of the road, but not the end of the scenery. The Devil's Garden trailhead just past the campground leads to some of the most interesting arches in the Park, including Landscape Arch, one of the longest natural arches in the world.

The relatively easy one-mile walk to Landscape Arch takes about 20 minutes, but it is important to stay on the well-constructed trail. Among the fascinating desert plant and animal life of Arches National Park is an especially fragile growth known as cryptogamic soil — a composition of several species of mosses, lichens, fungi and algae covering much of the terrain of untrampled desert areas. This covering protects against erosion and provides moisture and nutrients for other plant growth; if damaged, it takes years to restore itself and eradicate the scar of a footstep.

The Visitor Center at Arches National Park is open year-round. Educational displays help explain the intricate geology of the area and the processes of fin and arch formation.

Canyonlands National Park

The 24-mile drive to Dead Horse Point State Park also leads to a turn-off to the Island in the Sky section of Canyonlands National Park. Two rivers, the Colorado and the Green, have cut canyons nearly 2,000 feet into the earth to meet at Cataract Canyon and create the landscape that gives Canyonlands National Park its name. The Island in the Sky is a high bench-plateau rising above the confluence of these mighty streams and separating their canyons. The Park sprawls into majestic distances below Grand View Point at the southern tip of the Island in the Sky plateau. Layer upon layer of flat sedimentary rocks, exposed in sharp contrasting colors of rich reds, browns and creamy whites, glisten in the air's clarity.

A Visitor Center with hiking and camping information is located at the Island in the Sky entrance to Canyonlands National Park. Another Visitor Center and entrance to Canyonlands is located farther south and east in the Needles District, which may be reached by State Highway 211 from US 191 between Moab and Monticello. Services and supplies are available just outside the Needles District entrance to the Park at Needles Outpost. A few miles past the Needles District ranger station, the highway ends at Big Spring Canyon Overlook where a vast maze of meandering canyons and a wilderness of balanced rocks, fins, arches and monoliths swirl into the distance beyond.

To really see Canyonlands — to see the fantastic Druid or Angel arches, the rock art of ancient inhabitants or the flood-fluted walls of hidden grottos deep in the canyons — one must leave the automobile behind. Hiking, four-wheel driving, horseback riding, river rafting and flying are all ways to become more intimate with this indescribable terrain. Many competent guides and outfitters are available. For more information on trip arrangements and the natural history of Canyonlands, Visitor Centers are located in both Moab and Monticello in addition to the stations within the park.

Top: Looking into Canyonlands from Dead Horse State Park.
PAT O'HARA

Above: A mighty confluence — the Green River joins the muddy Colorado; Canyonlands National Park. FRED HIRSCHMANN

Opposite, top: The Green River and Canyonlands' White Rim. GARY LADD

Opposite, lower left: Moon and needles. FRANK S. BALTHIS

Opposite, lower right: A wilderness of rocks in Canyonlands' Needles District. ROBERT WINSLOW

Dead Horse Point State Park

An isolated island-mesa, Dead Horse Point offers spectacular mountain views and panoramas of Canyonlands National Park and the Colorado River 2,000 feet below. To the west, vertical walls of Wingate Formation Sandstone can be seen rimming the Island in the Sky section of Canyonlands National Park; due south, it is possible to see the White Rim Sandstone and Cedar Mesa Sandstones making up the Maze and the Needles sections of Canyonlands. Farther to the south, the Abajo Mountains can be seen rising behind Hatch Point. To the east, the prominent gray peaks of the La Sal Mountains are silhouetted along the skyline.

Old-time cowboys once used this point as a natural corral for capturing wild horses. After mustangs had been run across the narrow neck of land leading to the point, a quickly erected brush fence trapped them on the promontory. This remote, isolated mesa became known as Dead Horse Point when a band of horses trapped too long died of thirst.

A visitor center, museum and campground are located in the park. Recreational activities include hiking, photography and nature walks — all amid spectacular views.

Newspaper Rock

On the way to the Needles District entrance to Canyonlands National Park is Newspaper Rock State Historical Park. Petroglyphs etched into the veneer of desert varnish on Wingate Sandstone record 2,000 years of human history in the place the Navajos call "Tse' Hane'" — rock that tells a story. Prehistoric peoples, Indian tribes of recent centuries and even early explorers contributed to a rich rock tapestry of hunting figures, animals and mysterious designs — even hand and footprints. The petroglyph language is undeciphered, but its beauty and power is moving, as surely the prehistoric artists meant it to be. Near the rock is a pleasant creekside picnic and camping area. An interpretive guide is available for the nature trail that meanders 1/4 mile through a natural setting from the trailhead adjacent to Newspaper Rock.

Natural Bridges National Monument

Three natural bridges carved out of 225-million-year-old Cedar Mesa Sandstone are protected at Natural Bridges National Monument. The highest of these, Sipapu Bridge, arches 220 feet above the streambed, with a span of 268 feet. The names of the three bridges come from the Hopi language. *Sipapu* is a Hopi word for an opening into the spirit world. Owachomo Bridge takes its name from the distinctive rock mound nearby. Pictographs of dancing figures found in the area suggested the name for Kachina Bridge.

Different types of erosional processes are responsible for these samples of nature's architecture. Sipapu and Kachina Bridges were created by streambed erosion eventually working through narrow necks of land that had once separated switchbacks in the water course. Owachomo Bridge is a good example of weathering — rain, frost action and sandblasting wind erosion.

A scenic eight-mile drive beginning at the Visitor Center features views of the massive bridges; viewing platforms overlooking each bridge are located near parking areas. All three bridges are also connected by several miles of hiking trails.

The Visitor Center at Natural Bridges is open year-round and is powered by one

of the world's largest photovoltaic solar energy systems. Created by Presidential Proclamation on April 16, 1908, Natural Bridges was the first national monument to be established in the state of Utah.

Valley of the Gods

Located between State Highway 261 and US 163, the Valley of the Gods side trip is a 17-mile adventure through some of the most unusual natural sandstone sculptures in the area. A little off the beaten path, this photographer's paradise can easily be visited enroute to or from Natural Bridges National Monument.

Goosenecks

The four-mile spur of Highway 316 off State Highway 261 below the Valley of the Gods is definitely worth the drive out to the overlooks at Goosenecks State Park. Strong rivers have a tendency to entrench themselves deeply into broad sweeping patterns called "goosenecks" in the terraced landscape of the Southwest's Grand Circle. The canyon rim at Goosenecks State Park provides a perfect view of the San Juan River 1,000 feet below as it meanders through an impressive series of "gooseneck" switchbacks. These sweeping meanders cause the river to flow nearly six miles to make just one mile of headway westward.

Edge of the Cedars State Park and Museum

Just outside the town of Blanding, Utah, atop a ridge overlooking Westwater Canyon, are the ruins of an Anasazi village occupied from 750 AD to 1220 AD. The site of an ongoing excavation which began in the late 1960s reveals six distinct habitations and ceremonial complexes. Visitors are encouraged to walk among the ruins but should not climb on the walls. A modern museum features artistic and educational displays of cultural artifacts, an area observation room and an excellent video presentation about the Ancient Ones who once dwelt here near the feet of the Abajo Mountains.

Opposite: Newspaper Rock tells the stories of prehistoric peoples, passing Indian tribes and early explorers. ED COOPER

Opposite, below: Sipapu Bridge spans White Canyon, Natural Bridges National Monument. GARY LADD

Top: Sandstone sculptures in Valley of the Gods. RICHARD WESTON

Above: The San Juan River, deeply entrenched in The Goosenecks. FRED HIRSCHMANN

CHAPTER FIVE

Path of the Ancients

 Echoes of the Ancient Ones are felt throughout plateau country. From the silence of stone walls, powerful images of Fremont and Anasazi rock art speak of the imagination of vanished cultures. Isolated ruins — remote storage granaries, lonely dwellings and small communities — tell of creative and resourceful people struggling to survive in a difficult environment. In the magnificent remains of civilizations found at Mesa Verde, Hovenweep, Canyon de Chelly and Tsegi Canyon, voices from the past gather into their strongest choruses. Reverberations of their distant songs may still be sensed in the traditions and arts of present-day Native Americans. Visitors retracing the path of the ancients may find inspiration in lives of those who have lived in harmony with the challenging land of the Southwest's Grand Circle.

Opposite: Clouds above mesa-top Far View Ruins, Mesa Verde National Park. CHUCK PLACE

Above: Kiva entrances at Mesa Verde's Spruce Tree House. JEFF NICHOLAS

Mesa Verde National Park

Mesa Verde National Park, established by President Theodore Roosevelt in 1906, is the only national park dedicated to preserving works of prehistoric man. There are more than 4,000 known archeological sites within the park. Here on a high table of greenery amid the starkness of the Colorado Plateaus, the ancient Anasazi developed sophisticated irrigation systems to farm the mesa tops and built spectacular cliff cities in mesa-side alcoves. The story of the Anasazi told by still-standing remnants of their desert castles and cliff palaces stirs a sense of wonder: When did they come; how did they live; why did they leave? Standing amid the peaceful beauty of the mesa with wide panoramic views of the Four

and were used for social, ritual and ceremonial purposes. By 1200 AD the Anasazi were building complex pueblo structures on the mesa and living in towns, but for unknown reasons they returned with their advanced building techniques and materials to the alcoves in the cliffs. Here, their architectural skills reached highest development in large apartment complexes complete with towers, plazas and great kivas built in the inaccessible faces of the mesa's rim. Only a few generations later, suddenly and mysteriously, the Anasazi left the Mesa Verde never to return.

A series of detailed dioramas and artifacts displayed in the natural history museum at Mesa Verde recreate visions of Anasazi life for park visitors. Implements for farming corn, beans and squash; hunting weapons; articles of clothing; baskets, pottery and other utensils; and ornaments made from feathers of domesticated turkeys and imported parrots, bones and gems give mute testimony to the vanished existence of a complex and highly organized society.

A short path from the museum leads to Spruce Tree House, an excellent example of an Anasazi cliff city with a kiva that may still be entered. Near the museum, two six-mile loops of the Ruins Road offer views of many more impressive cliff dwellings, mesa top structures, archeological excavations and irrigation works. The Mesa Top Loop visits sites emphasizing the full range of Anasazi life on the mesa — pithouse hamlets, Sun Point Pueblo, Sun Temple, Fire Temple and an overlook of Mesa Verde's centerpiece, Cliff Palace. The Cliff Palace Loop connects views of Balcony House and numerous other cliff dwellings. Today a steep path and four 10-foot ladders replace the hand and foot holds of the Anasazi down the mesa rim to Cliff Palace.

From the Far View Visitor Center, a 12-mile scenic drive to Wetherill Mesa explores ruins on the western plateaus of the park. A free mini-train loop connects overviews and trails. The National Park Service offers interpretive ranger-led hikes to several of Mesa Verde National Park's principal sites. Mesa-top Far View Lodge offers the only lodging within the park; camping is also available in spacious Morefield Campground.

Above: Oak Tree House, nestled in a mesa-rim alcove, Mesa Verde National Park. DAN PEHA

Opposite, top: Natural water basin and pitcher once used by Hovenweep's inhabitants. JERRY JACKA

Opposite, below: Afternoon lights and shadows at Mesa Verde's Cliff Palace. DAN PEHA

Corners area of Utah, Colorado, Arizona and New Mexico, it is impossible not to contemplate the mystery of their departure and what life must have been like ages ago on the Mesa Verde.

Archeological research has traced several stages in the development of the Anasazi civilization through architectural ruins found on Mesa Verde. When these people first arrived in the region around 500 AD, they sought shelter in cliff alcoves and overhangs. Later, they scraped pithouses out of the earth on the mesa top and covered them with brush. Around 900 AD, the Anasazi began to develop new masonry techniques and started building structures and living above ground, though the old-style pit-houses were still used for storage and winter residences. Eventually, as surface living extended year-round, the subterranean chambers became known as "kivas"

Hovenweep
National Monument

Twenty-five miles of graded dirt road complete the drive to the six complexes of pueblo ruins stradling the Utah and Colorado borders at Hovenweep National Monument. These remote ruins are remarkable for their number of standing towers and castle-like walls set atop and among dramatic rock formations against scenic backdrops of clear plateau country skies. A self-guiding trail beginning at the ranger station leads through the prehistoric ruins of the Square Tower Group. Other ruins are connected by a network of unpaved roads and trails. There is camping at the monument, but no other accommodations or supplies are available.

Right: Canyon de Chelly's White House, at the base of towering varnished cliffs. LOU SWENSON

Inset: The coming of the white man is shown in pictographs at Canyon del Muerto. TOM BEAN

Below: Spider Rock, Canyon de Chelly National Monument. JERRY JACKA

Opposite, above: Wind-sculpted dunes and Monument Valley's West Mitten. CHUCK PLACE

Opposite, below: Petroglyphs and "The Sun's Eye" at Monument Valley Navajo Tribal Park. JERRY JACKA

Canyon De Chelly National Monument

The name "De Chelly" is a Spanish corruption of the Navajo word "Tsegi" which means "rock canyon." In Canyon de Chelly National Monument, present-day Navajos live, herd and farm in the traditional ways along tree-shaded waters. Above them — nestled at the bases of towering red sandstone cliffs — ancient ruins of a once-thriving civilization reflect slanting sunlight from beyond the canyon's rim. Anasazi peoples occupied Canyon de Chelly for almost 1,000 years before their unexplained disappearance in the 13th century. Today, the ruins of their fantastic structures stand silent and empty, while spirals of smoke from log and earth Navajo homes called "hogans" and the sounds of flocks drift and echo up the sheer 1,000 feet of the canyon walls.

Canyon de Chelly's South Rim and North Rim Drives, each about 36 miles round trip, take in a total of 12 overlooks of the canyons and ruins including First Ruin, Junction Ruin, Antelope House, Mummy Cave Ruin and Spider Rock — a sandstone spire rising 800 feet from the canyon floor. White House Ruin, the best-known Anasazi cliff dwelling in the canyon, may be reached by a 2½-mile round-trip trail from White House Overlook. For other ventures into the canyon, a guide and free permit are required; four-wheel drive tours led by knowledgable and informative Navajo guide-drivers are available.

Cottonwood Campground near park headquarters is well-shaded and has fireplaces, tables and restrooms. Meals, comfortable accommodations, Native American arts and crafts and various canyon tours are available at nearby Thunderbird Lodge.

Monument Valley Tribal Park

In Monument Valley, Navajos living in octagonal hogans made of cedar logs from the higher mesas and red earth of the valley floor continue traditional arts of rug-weaving and jewelry-making amid some of the most photogenic landscape on earth. The towering buttes, monuments and spires of Monument Valley perform glowing color changes and long shadow dances across the valley floor as the sun rises and sets each day in the incredibly picturesque land of the Navajo. It is no surprise that many films — including John

Wayne's "Stagecoach" — were made during Hollywood's heyday of Westerns on location here in Monument Valley.

Limited automobile travel on the dirt roads of the tribal park is possible, but for the most intimate visits to the valley's grandeur and to be invited into a Navajo home, it is well worth taking a tour with Navajo guides who have lived their lives in close communion with this land. These friendly guides know the old and modern names of every formation, the habits of the wildlife and the customs and stories of the old ways, and they are also very helpful with photography tips.

Tour arrangements may be made at Goulding's Trading Post and Lodge where guest rooms are strategically situated to take advantage of valley views in the changing light. The trading post, homesteaded in 1923 by Harry Goulding and his wife "Mike," is an historic site where Navajos continue to trade. It was Harry Goulding who first introduced Monument Valley to John Wayne and award-winning film-maker John Ford.

A campground, hospital and market are also located near the trading post. Monument Valley Tribal Park is located on the Navajo Reservation and is operated and administered by the people of the Navajo nation.

Above: Navajo girls in traditional velveteen, near Monument Valley's Totem Pole formation.
MAGGIE McLAREN

Left: Gouldings Lodge and Trading Post overlooks the splendid Monument Valley scenery.
GARY LADD

Opposite, top: A Navajo hogan, Monument Valley Navajo Tribal Park. LOU SWENSON

Opposite, bottom: Betatakin ruin, Navajo National Monument. GARY LADD

Navajo National Monument

Betatakin, Keet Seel and Inscription House, three of the best-preserved and most elaborate cliff dwellings known, are located in the Tsegi Canyons of Navajo National Monument. The Visitor Center at Navajo National Monument contains excellent displays about Anasazi life including a walk-in replica of a cliff dwelling. Though Inscription House is presently closed due to urgent stabilization needs and trips to Keet Seel require planning, the half-mile Sandal Trail from the monument's Visitor Center leads to an impressive overlook of the 135-room Betatakin cliff dwelling. For closer looks at Betatakin, three-hour ranger-led hikes descending 700 feet into the canyon can be scheduled May through September. The eight-mile trail to Keet Seel, where a 160-room complex with six ceremonial kivas fills a gigantic alcove in the Navajo Sandstone, takes a full day of hiking or horseback riding. Permits and advance registration are necessary; Navajo guides and horses are available. Keet Seel is open Memorial Day weekend through Labor Day.